Chapter i

INTRODUCTION

For more than three decades, Afghanistan has been a nation torn by endless war and conflict (Goodson, 2001). Scholars have always considered Afghanistan a traditional conservative society. And as history has proven time and again, women and children are the most disadvantaged sections of the population in conflict situations (Barakat and Wardell, 2002).

Between 1979 and 1989, the Soviet Union invaded Afghanistan. After years of conflict, when Russia withdrew from the country, civil war erupted between tribes and lasted between the years 1989 and 1996. Conflict has been a ceaseless aspect of social life in Afghanistan. During the Taliban regime that followed post 1996, human rights violations peaked due to their conservative interpretation of the Shar'ia law. But women and children were perhaps the most affected by these restrictions by the Taliban. Heavy sanctions were placed on what Afghan women and children could and could not do. Post the murder of Ahmad Shah Massoud (who fought the Taliban) and the 9/11 twin tower attack, the US declared war on Afghanistan (BBC, 2010).

With constant conflict ongoing in the country, the number of war-widows and orphaned children in the country rose sharply. Refugee movement rose drastictly and so did the number of camps in Iran and Pakistan (Baitenmann, 1990)

Inside the country there were no schools for girl children, many boys were pulled out from school due to various reasons such as poverty, refugee movement and security situation. Play and laughter were heavily policed. (Skaine, 2002)

Today, many parts of Afghanistan are free of the Taliban regime but post-conflict reconstruction of social life is a painfully slow process - especially for the children of Afghanistan, the future of the nation. Some of the biggest problems faced by children in conflict zones are exposure to landmines, internal displacement and refugee movement, disability, poverty, lack of health-care and education, child labour, sexual abuse, malnutrition and the grave danger of being recruited as child soldiers. (Machel, 1996)

Rebuilding Afghanistan and aiding the children of this country to be self-sufficient and responsible citizens is a process that has been the focus of many international aid agencies. While conducting this research, it became apparent that the international media often tend to marginalize the voices of children and represent them mainly in the context of victims of war and violence. There is little to no child specific content in Afghanistan's mainstream media. There are scattered initiatives by various NGOs to produce child-specific media, but it remains amongst a small group of beneficiaries.

The purpose of this research is to enable the children of Afghanistan to critically evaluate their role in the Afghan public sphere and then develop an alternative media space – a magazine, in this case. This space would then be used as a tool to help define new meanings and significations of the children's rapidly changing identities.

The UN report on impact of armed conflict of children suggests that peace-building education should include the use of media to aid in the eventual reconciliation of the shattered society. "Both the content and process for education should promote peace, social justice, respect for human rights and the acceptance of responsibility. Children need to learn skills of negotiation, problem solving, critical thinking and communication that will enable them to resolve conflicts without resorting to violence," it recommends (Machel, 1996).

One of the biggest factors that govern the childrens' perception of the war, peace-building and reconstruction efforts is from the media. Media is suggested as one of the most important tools in peace-building. While the media is often criticised as being a tool that propagates violence, other scholars have recognised the immense potential that the media presents in the areas of community reconciliation and democracy-building. (Lemish and Gotz, 2007)

"It can be an instrument of conflict resolution, when the information it presents is reliable, respects human rights, and represents diverse views. It's the kind of media that upholds accountability and exposes malfeasance. It's the kind of media that enables a society to make well-informed choices, which is the precursor of democratic governance. It is a media that reduces conflict and fosters human security." (Ross, 2002)

Media for children in conflict zones can be used to facilitate peace-building, mutual understanding, prejudice reduction and conflict-resolution amongst other more important functions as expressing themselves and understanding how people in their own societies and other societies feel about conflict. Children should be considered as serious potential participants of the public sphere, who require a lot more attention from the media.

One of the ways to do this would be to develop participatory programs for children in the form of news, informative and edutainment genres. (Lemish and Gotz, 2007).

The aim of this study is to allow Afghan children from five different provinces create their own alternative media space by means of a children's magazine and understand how they define and view children's media and it's role in their lives.

Chapter ii
Literature Review
In focussing on analytical framework for the alternative media development project, this literature review is divided into two parts.

- Theoretical perspectives in Alternative and Community Media
- A review of two community media projects in post-conflict territories

Though there are a number of children's projects in conflict and post-conflict zones around the world, there is very little documented literature available on these kinds of projects. The projects chosen bear close resemblance to this initiative with regards with content and structure.

Theoretical perspectives in Alternative and Community Media:

Community and Alternative media are situated within discourses encompassing socio-political hegemony concerning imperialistic media and marginalised critiques of deliberative democracy (Madrid et al cited in Clemencia, 2001)

a) The origins of Community Media:
In the 1970s, debates raged in UN councils regarding the under-representation of developing nations with regards to what they liked to term 'communication injustices'. The Macbride report would term these 'Communication Injustices' as dominant flow of information and communication content from the first world countries to the third world countries. (Clemencia, 2001)

Clemencia further notes that most of this content originated either from the US or the rich Western European countries. This caused alarm to the policy makers and leaders from the third-world. Two main reasons were attributed to this. One was the potential corrosion national identities via constant exposure to western media content and the second the deterioration of their own local media industries.

To counter these issues and to promote information flows between developing nations or what was she terms as 'south-to-south communication', several attempts at establishing local news agencies were made. However, none of these attempts worked due to lack of 'co-ordination, capacity and quality.'

To be able to address these concerns, the United Nations proposed the New World Information and Communication Order (NWICO). A norm that aimed to create more balance in international news flows. Post the 'Many Voices, One World' by Macbride, the NWICO was welcome. However, with further debates and discussions, the USA decided to withdraw citing that the NWICO hindered the free-flow of communication. Other countries like the UK followed suit. (Carlsson, 2005)

Despite these efforts, the capitalistic media conglomerates of the west began growing in size. This kind of dominant corporate media from the west influenced the social, political, economic and cultural life of the recipient countries. Eventually, it created a phenomenon that Tomlison (2001) terms 'Media Imperialism'.

"The hegemony of (these) dominant media institutions in shaping public opinion, championing neo-liberal economics, cultivating a consumer culture, and fashioning domestic and international communication policy undermine(d) the legitimacy, let alone the viability of community media initiatives" (Bower et al cited in Clemencia, 2001).

To challenge these discourses, emerging out of a need to assert the voice of the locals and represent the ethnic and marginalised was born what we now term 'Alternative media and Community Media'.

"In the light of the growing influence of transnational media corporations in the production and distribution of news, information, and culture, community media have enormous relevance within the emerging global political and cultural economy. In absence of plurality of voices, opinions and perspectives available in mainstream media, people across the global have taken it upon themselves to appropriate communication technologies in an effort to enlarge the terms of public discourse, secure a space for local cultural expression and

enhance participatory democracy on local, national, regional and
international." (Hamelink,1994).

b) Whose Public Sphere?
Howley (2005) argues that "while the Alternative media space promised to
offer accurate, in-depth and progressive coverage, the production quality and
ethical frameworks associated with it were hugely flawed. However, he adds,
from a Habermasian perspective, it did seem to provide a platform for the
marginalised to engage in debate and democracy.

Habermas' (1962) normative public sphere theory argues that a healthy
public sphere is the basis of a healthy civil society. The ability to solve issues
in public life, according to Habermas depended on the ability of the citizens
to engage in discursive practice and participation in large numbers.

The Habermasian public sphere envisions equal participation and the will to
be able to deliberate together and ultimately, achieve political action as an
outcome.

While this would have and should have been the theoretical framework that
dominated the western media ideology, many of these agencies emerged from
a tradition of capitalism and one that worked only towards profits. In trying
to achieve those goals, the majorities were required to be given more content
space than the minorities who were both intentionally and unintentionally
marginalised and suppressed. (Howley, 2005)

A number of critics to this Habermasian model were put forth and notably the
ones by feminist theorists such as Mouffe (1988) and Nancy Fraser (1990),
questioning the several gaps such as the conceptions of private and public,
the role of women and the minorities, the rhetoric of the 'common concern',
'hegemonic dominance' and 'exclusion' (as cited in Howley, 2005) amongst
the citizens.

However, these seem true of the global media space too. Hegemonic
discourses developed, home and foreign news covered differently, minorities
were not given their rightful space and the 'common good' was often
manufactured in accordance to the requirements of the institutions that

controlled the economy. (Dueze, 2006)

When the technology for alternative media spaces became more and more widely available, the production of messages that addressed these exact issues was born. In other words, several traditions of 'Development Communication' were born around the world. Some of the main schools were the Bretton Wood School, The Latin American School, The Indian School, The African School, Los Banos school and the Participatory Development Communication School. (Manyozo, 2006)

Manyozo further explains, that the Bretton Wood school addressed economic strategies to lift communities out of poverty. This mainly used ready-to-fit projects that didn't really find place in the way the capitalistic environment of the west wanted it to. However, the other schools of development communication that emerged thereafter in different parts of the world emphasized the use of horizontal two-way communication in Freirian theory. They went on to term the community members 'stakeholders' in the process rather than 'beneficiaries' or audiences. (Besette, 2004)

However, while community media initiatives and participatory communication techniques gained prominence both in the public realm and within the organizational structure of the UN, a dichotomous debate on whether this kind of participatory media really did any good raged amongst the intellectuals. While the fall of the NWICO was criticised, several scholars, according to Clemencia (2001) note that "the alternative media debate should take a new course and contribute towards democratization of the public sphere."

"The imperialist top-down communication initiatives were sought to be quashed and newer discourses of locality were expected to be created." However, western media was still considered the 'powerful' and the local media deemed 'powerless' (Clemencia, 2001)

Some other theorists such as Kaplun the aim of alternative and community media should not be one that seeks to compete with western media. He argues that the real goal is "not to solve the world's unbalanced info flows, but to strengthen popular organisation and mobilization."(as cited in

Clemencia, 2001)

Clemencia, however, considers a different perspective with regards to the binary notions of power relations. He suggests that alternative media should relook power dynamics and consider how power equations between a number of different players in the local community and the community at large is being shaped / changed because of alternative media presence. He argues that power is not something that is a constant and that the positions of power vary in continuum.

Revisiting the arguments of Mouffe and Fraser, it is evident that minorities still had to struggle to have their voices heard. Despite the developments in alternative and community media, the problem of representing all segments of the society in a Habermasian perspective persisted.

This brings us to the question of where children fit in. Are children considered citizens? As part of the Habermasian public sphere? Can they assert their space? What is the meaning of children's media in development communication? What place does it have in the media universe? How do children and adults perceive it? And how democratic or deliberative can it actually be?

While there is little literature available on what the role of children in public sphere and in this case, the alternative media sphere, let us examine two projects conducted in Bosnia and Gaza to try and find answers to these questions

c) Children's Media in Conflict Zones

While there seems to be very little space for children to participate in the public sphere, the situation is only worse in conflict and post-conflict zones. Gotz and Lemish both recommend alternative and community media as an effective tool in peace-building. It is vital they argue, to include children in these ventures, not just because they are the future citizens of the nation-state, but also because, they are a means of intervention themselves.

"Children are seen as a means of intervention, whether it is through education, psychological interventions, or information and entertainment via the media. What media scholars are interested in is looking at where those things intersect." (2007)

This is an interesting question raised by Lemish. Where does children's media in conflict zones intersect with education and entertainment? How can a largely ignored minority such as children challenge official discourses and be given spaces in the fragmented public sphere to create personal narratives of their imagined experiences?

With technology and access largely restricted, freedom of speech predominantly non-existant, children, are treated as threats in public spaces – in terms of their own safety and projected vulnerability to their adults (Roozemond and Wenzel, 2002).

Gotz and Lemish (2007) argue, "Children are much more aware of current social conflicts and events than we may think and they want the media to value and address their questions, concerns and needs."

These findings demand creating alternative media spaces for children where they can express their voices, address their needs, answer their questions and define their representations. While there are a number of projects in conflict and post-conflict zones that try to address these issues, few are documented and critically reviewed.

Here, we look at two projects to understand the dynamics of alternative media for children in conflict and post-conflict zones.

d) Bookmaking Project in Bosnia:

"This project was conducted for pre-adolescents in Serbian and Bosnian girls at a summer camp outside Sarajevo, Bosnia in 2005. During this camp, children from Bosnia, Serbia and Croatia were brought together by the Global Children's Organisation to engage in variety of activities, including conflict, resolution, art, athletics and academics.. The literacy workshops that were offered gave the children the opportunity to write, illustrate and construct their own books about topics such as peace, friendship and the preservation of nature in Bosnia." (Darvin, 2009)

Taking a deeper look at Darvin's paper it appears that the children really enjoyed the project and made were able to form friendships with other participants not belonging to their own ethnicity. An earlier research, Darvin quotes in her paper suggests that children from rival ethnicities strongly believed that it was impossible to reconcile differences and it was best for different communities to remain in their communal groups.

She cites two studies conducted in Bosnia and Herzegovina about culture, ethnic conflict and moral orientation of children. Children were presented fables with animal personifications and questioned on how the characters could reconcile their differences. One child said, "The ox and the dog should go with other oxes and dogs. So they don't fight. They are not the same… The ox is not able to speak dog language, so wouldn't be able to understand each other."

This very insightful observation speaks volumes of how these children perceived children from other communities.

Yet at the end of the project on of the girls said, "Friendship is a wonderful thing. I hang out with children from 'other parts of the world' We understand our different languages. We are so different, but we hang out together very nicely and we try to make peace."

While the success quotient of this project seems phenomenal, it is one that has been initiated by external stimulus. In an ideal public sphere, as Habermas would argue, the children as subjects of the public sphere were not "insulated from the deleterious influence of state and commercial interests".

While it would be erroneous term the project co-ordinators of ones with commercial interests, they do have an interest, possibly propelled by bilateral donors in the welfare of the nation. It is beyond the scope of this review to debate what these intentions were. However, the fact remains that they were indeed external influences.

Darvin writes, "The bookmaking project was 'created' with the intention of helping the children… interact with children from other religious and ethnic backgrounds in a non-threatening academic environment, allowing them to explore the concepts of peace and friendship…"

It is clear that, the project went with a pre-conceived goal. While they might have been honourable intentions, the fact remains that the children are made to think the way the international development agency wants them to think. This would carry very little difference from all the indoctrination that they have been facing since childhood about other ethnicities.

e) Digital Story-telling Workshop in Gaza

The "Re-imagining Project" (Sawhney, 2010) is a program of digital video, photography and storytelling workshops that supports Palestinian children and youth in expressing their cultural identity, personal narratives, and creative visions through participatory digital media.

The project consisted of conducting Training of Trainers (ToT) sessions in Ramallah and Gaza and conducting digital storytelling workshops in collaboration with community centres in Al Aroub camp in the West Bank and Jabaliya camp in Gaza.

While this project promises to be more participatory in nature than the previous project which assumed what was good for the children, these words still disseminate dominant discourses of being suggestive in terms of telling them to think about conflict.

The initiative, while proving to be an excellent way to help the children speak and represent themselves, was not something that was conceived by them as a way to come to terms with their lives.

This workshop though, doesn't suggest to the children, unlike the previous example where the children were explicitly suggested what to think (about).

The workshop involved a number of focus groups that placed high importance on the opinions of the participants and spoke in great detail their experiences of war.

f) Children and discourses of war:

It is the assumption that most of the children in conflict affected contexts seem to want to speak about war that should perhaps be problematized.

Both these examples, as well as alternative media projects around the world, prompt the participants to relate their experiences of conflict in implicit ways. Do the participants want to be reminded of this? Both these projects seem to ignore that question.

The Reimagining Gaza project, did exactly the same with the very first focus group speaking about the participant's experiences of war and life in a refugee camp. The topic of the focus group almost forces the participant to think and speak about it. There are ethical questions involved here. While they might be willing and forthcoming in their accounts, would they really speak about their experiences if the facilitator had not been a 'foreigner' who actively sought these answers?

While these kinds of questions need deeper deliberation, the fact remains that alternative media in conflict and post-conflict zones, almost always only focus on the 'conflict' itself.

The films that came out of the digital story-telling workshop all focused on conflict. The stories that came out of the bookmaking project focused on friendship (rather than enmity created by war). While it is undeniable that the daily universe of these children are inhabited by these very images, would they perhaps want to be exposed to content that non-conflict affected children around the world enjoy and seek?

While it is important that these issues are addressed, there seems to be a big void in the alternative media universe that addresses any of the other kinds of content and needs that children, just as children, would like to experience.

It seems like we, the development and media practitioners, who often lead recovery and peace-building missions refuse to acknowledge the fact that alternative media spaces need to allow children to express discourses of not just their lives in the context of conflict, but also in other contexts of general and imagined childhood.

Since not many studies have been done addressing these issues, this research would try to find answers to these very questions.

g) Are we missing something?

This research explores the many connotations of self-representation by the children of Afghanistan by means of a participatory media project that gives them an opportunity to quash mainstream media's discourses of them and create an alternative media space.

From the reviewed literature, it is evident that children hardly have a space in the public sphere and especially in conflict and post-conflict environments. Scholars argue that children play a vital role in peace-building and reconstruction and they need to be given their rightful space in the media-sphere.

However, what has been observed is that there are very few documented, well-planned out alternative media projects that are specifically designed for children. For children in conflict zones, the focus remains mainly coming to terms with the conflict surrounding their lives. There has been little work done on allowing children to represent themselves from other perspectives.

This study aims to find out exactly what these perspectives are.

This project emerged out of a request from children's Shura-e-Atfals (children's parliament) in schools across the country, the children expressed a need for an alternate media space to express themselves, address their issues and connect with other children in more remote parts of the country who have little or no access to any kind of media. Born out of those conversations was the magazine 'Zank Tafrih' (The Break). A space where children voice out their opinions and create content that (they would like to) represents their lives.

The question I am attempting to probe into is how children in conflict zones understand media. Does it always necessarily have to do with conflict related issues? Are there other areas that they would rather concentrate on? What are the experiences of these children with reference to their media environments? How would they change and if they would want to add or delete aspects of it.

In a media-scape like Afghanistan, where there is very little high quality programming available for children, the study tried to understand what kind of content they relate to and felt the need for. Hence, the aim of this research is to

To engage with the children of Afghanistan and understand how they look at and define children's media and its role in their lives

The study used participatory action research as a methodology to seek answers for this question, while developing a children's magazine (as requested by the children). A parallel workshop on community radio was also being carried out at the same time.

This project places a lot of importance on the views of the children and pushed them to critically think about the reasons for each and every decision they made. It was an insightful experience both for the research / facilitator and the participants.

The final magazine is to be distributed to 10,000 children across Afghanistan (In five provinces). The evaluation stage of this project is yet to happen. But, that is beyond the scope of this dissertation.

Chapter iii

Research Design and Methodology:

This participatory research project was commissioned by Afghan Educational Circus for Children, an Afghan grass-root NGO that focuses on creating live entertainment to educate children in different parts of the country on issues such as peace-building, landmine awareness, gender equality, child rights and health and hygiene.

While the project required the development of alternate media space for Afghan children, the best possible approach for such a project from media development literature appeared to be Participatory Communication Development. This approach is derived as an offshoot of the Participatory Action Research methodology.

a) Communication for development: Perspectives

In the late 50s and early 60s, development practitioners recognised the importance of communication initiatives and began implementing it in their development projects. During the 70s, a number of projects began to fail and the reason attributed were top-down communication models. The stress lay on implementing pre-identified development initiatives without giving much attention to the process of development itself. (Mefalopulos, 2003).

The three key areas identified for these failures according to Hornik (1988) were theory failtures that falsely assumed certain development problems were linked with certain solutions and inadequately designed projects and lack of condusive environments.

Other researchers have identified project failures as residing in "poor formulation and planning, inadequate design, insufficient understanding of local realities, use of inappropriate technology, ineffective training methodologies and lack of enabling policies" (Anyaegbunam 1998, Hornik, 1988)

These theoretical perspectives lead us to conclude more involvement from the local community or the local 'stakeholders' would yield better results. One of the other big problems faced by the International NGO community was sustaining the few successful development initiatives. Foreign capacity-builders often left the location after a certain period of time and once successful projects began dwindling in the absence of experts. Hence it became important to capacity-build local human resources to implement sustainable projects (Jaffe, 1998).

In the late 50s and 60s, theorists such as Laswell (1948), Lerner (1958) and Schramm (1964) put forth theories on communicating national development. However, this was done with a perspective that the kind of development sought by the third world depended on the dominant 'modernity paradigm' that advocated values such as liberal democracy, free market trade, capitalism, industrialisation and science (Melkote, 1991).

Moreover, these models only advocated a top-down approach of communication were based on persuasion as the core conceptual framework. These linear models of communication, however yielded little results when applied to development communication as they failed to address the real issues that concerned the communities. Further, they often tended to exert the western notions of liberation and modernity into the underdeveloped / developing environments. This proved problematic to the communities which was often accustomed to very different social, economic and political institutions.

"From the 1970s and onwards, voices of both development practitioners and academics from developing countries have raised fundamental questions about the Western domination of the work and debate in development. The questions include who voices the concerns of the poorest and most marginalized populations..." (Tufte and Mefalopulos, 2009)

To counter these arguments, models such as the Innovation-Dissemination model (Everett, 1962) that focussed on a three-step communication process that identified a target population, an innovation message to be transmitted to them and a channel to do so. While the previous models were focussed more on mass media information dissemination, Everette's model focussed on community media. However, there were several criticisms to this including the model's lack of ability to take into account the pluralistic nature of the audience and also the social, political and economic background of the ground.

While all of these models focussed on the top-down approach, there a clear lack of any kind of horizontal or bottom-up communcation amongst the stakeholders themselves (Besette, 2004).

Freire (1973) and several other communicators after him, identified communication as a process that is inseparable from the social and political processes necessary for development.(Besette, 2004)

Friere's model, as introduced in his book the 'Pedagogy of the Oppressed', argues how real development would mean allowing the community to involve themselves in every stage of the development process. This would typically involve researching to identify development issues, designing a participatory approach to solving the issue at hand, implementing the design and evaluating the outcome of the initiative. (1997)

This approach, apart from being able to mirror an environment of full democracy, also fosters a context for some of the following:

The participatory approach allows the community to take charge of their own development problems and feel responsible for it, ensures the use of indigenous knowledge and expertise, allows freedom from external professionals, makes sure the right issues are addressed and alleviates the sense of powerlessness and alienation. (White, 1982 as cited in Mefalupulos, 2003)

b) Why participatory communication?

Participatory Communication was used in this research as a means of attempting to gain an understanding of what the children of Afghanistan considered an appropriate media space and its role in their lives. As a media practitioner, creating a magazine (the alternate media space) just using any of the other communication models except the participatory communication model would have meant giving the children a space that the researcher, a subject influenced by Western ideals, envisioned as appropriate, but not necessarily something that the children might relate with. This was the core reason for choosing the participatory media approach.

Like most short-term development projects, this one had a specific time frame of three-weeks. Other methodological approaches such as ethnography could've been used to observe what the children's lifestyles and environments and hence derive what would be most appropriate for them in terms of content. But the time-frame was too short to carry out any kind of ethnographic study.

But a more befitting and pertinent methodological approach seemed to lie in participatory communication. Since this approach would allow the children to voice their opinions, define their representations and think about their lives as conflict affected subjects, it won hands down over other approaches. As a foreign facilitator with very little knowledge of the actual social, political and economic circumstance of the nation-state, it was only appropriate that the children led me, the researcher and facilitator in the process of creating the media space rather than me leading them.

c) Sampling:

Fourteen children from five different provinces participated in the participatory communication workshop to develop Zangat Afri. All the children were already part of the organisation's activities involving performing arts in various development and peacebuilding projects. All the children were betweeen the ages 10 and 16. Since children start school only at the age of 7 in Afghanistan, the youngest readers were assumed to be at least 10 years old.

The children selected to attend the workshop were chosen by means of a 'Shura' (parliament) where a children's election appointed representatives from each of the provinces to attend the workshop.

There were children participants from Kabul, Herat, Jalalabad, Nangahar and Ghor provinces of Afghanistan. While the NGO operated in 16 Afghan provinces, transporting children different provinces to Kabul city proved a huge logistical and security challenge. Secure transportation / roads were only available from the above provinces. In a conflict zone, with ongoing peacekeeping operations, we had to be content with allowing children only from five provinces to decide how children from all over Afghanistan would want to be represented. However, the workshop included children from Nangahar, a Pashto speaking province as opposed to all the other children from Dari speaking provinces.

While there were equal number of girls and boys, most of the girls hailed from Kabul province. Two girls from Herat province participated in the workshop. In a country that is one of the most oppressive in the world for women's rights, young girls are not allowed to leave their homes. However, since Herat is a province from which flying (rather than by road) to Kabul makes more logistic sense, the girl children were allowed to attend.

d) Sampling drawbacks:

In a current conflict zone such as Afghanistan, the project had to be content with having as many children from the rural areas as possible. While the gender balance was maintained, there were more children from Kabul than from the provinces. Child participants from Kabul typically exhibited more liberal tendencies than the children from the rural areas. Also, during the course of the workshop, it was observed that children from the rural areas gave more references to crime and violence than the children from the city did. The content of the resulting magazine and hence this research might be skewed to be more 'modern' in its representation than Afghanistan really is, because of the sampling. The imagined identities of the urban children tended to lean towards western sensibilities while the imagined identities of the children from the provinces touched the ones of the children residing in Kabul. For instance, girls from the city only used a scarf to cover their heads, while the girls from Heart used a skullcap and a hijab to cover their heads. By the end of the three weeks, the Herati girls were trying to emulate the Kabul girls by only wearing a headscarf. This simple observation and yet it demonstrates how a layered imitation cycle would influence the content of the final product.

e) Research Design:

My role as facilitator was only limited to empowering the participants to think in every step of the process. The entire process consisted of five steps:
- Conception of the idea
- Needs Assessment
- Strategy design
- Implementation
- Evaluation

For the purposes of this research question, we will only look the first three steps of the participatory process. As participatory media theorists advocate, the process involved a lot of horizontal communication.

f) The participants:

The facilitator (Me – A foreigner with very little knowledge of the local language, Dari)
16 child participants (Boys and girls from five provinces aged between 10-16) - Appendix 2
One adult male and adult female Afghan staff to ensure inappropriate mixing of genders didn't occur within the workshop settings (Their role was predominantly passive – however, the children discussed their ideas with them every now and then)
The interpreter (Male, aged 16) was also one of the participants.

g) The setting:

The workshop was conducted in a well-ventilated room where the participants sat in a semi-circle facing the facilitator. The participants tended to group themselves with their own sex and sit on opposite sides, for purposes of fluid communication amongst the participants, sometimes the participants were asked to mix with the members of the opposite sex while doing some of the some of the group activities. Initially, it proved difficult to get the girls and boys to mix and express themselves with each other. The culture of Afghanistan doesn't allow unmarried girls to speak to members of the opposite sex. While the same applied for boys, it was much relaxed and tended to be overlooked as 'male tendency'. The senior female staff while initially apprehensive of allowing the girls mix with the boys, got used to the idea in a couple of days and justified it by saying that they were only working together and Islam, the religion of the land, allowed it.

h) Structure of the workshop:

In adherence to the core principles of participatory action research, the participants defined the goals of the workshop. The role of the facilitator was to introduce participatory process and encourage interpersonal communication to encourage finding common ground in achieving the five steps lined out above.

Here, as Freire argues, the participants were 'stakeholders' rather than 'beneficiaries'. The facilitator, the NGO, the donor and the target audience and the government were all 'stakeholders' in this initiative as they all have equal interest in the success of the project as the participants themselves. Besides, the process itself proves as a learning ground for all the stakeholders involved.

In Freire's perspective, "This kind of communication means moving from a focus on facilitating exchanges between different stakeholders to address a common problem. This could lead to a common development initiative to experiment with possible solutions and to identify what is needed to support the initiative in terms of partnership, knowledge and material conditions." (as cited in Bessette, 2007)

Each day the workshop was conducted for four hours: 10 am to 12 pm and 2pm to 4pm.
All discussions were two-way, horizontal communication. In many cases, children worked in mixed groups. The sizes of the groups varied activity to activity.

Please see appendix 3 for detailed explanation of the workshop schedule.

I) Workshop schedule:

Week	Activity
Week 1	During the first part of the week, the focus was on getting to know each other and also getting used to opening up to a foreign facilitator. We did this by means of a number of games. Later, the children spoke about their favourite media content and what they liked and didn't like about it.
Week 2	The participants accomplished three major tasks this week. They analysed a number of photos of Afghan children from the international media and thought about the issue of representation, they defined how they would change it and what they considered good media content to represent the children of Afghanistan. And towards the end of the week, the participants, having thought and discussed these issues, came up with a name for the magazine that would kick-started the process of creating the magazine itself.
Week 3	Keeping the activities of week 3 in mind, the participants worked in groups to draw up a list of content ideas. The final contents were determined by means of a vote. The latter half of the week saw the children working on creating the content of the magazine. One of the main features of the workshop was the story-writing session. The resulting story created by the children gives a lot of insights into their lives and expectations. More of this will be discussed in the next session. The children did interviews, reportages, clicked pictures and worked on aggregating the rest of the content
Week 4	The facilitator, in a pedagogic two-way process, worked with the participants in enabling them to think about the basic principles of journalism. This included sessions on newsgathering, writing, editing, representation and ethics. These sessions were applied to the content-generation and simultaneously, the design process. However, the children were unable to fully-participate in the design process as would've been ideal due to lack of resources. However their inputs were taken in and applied to the designing process as best as possible.

Chapter iv

Results and Interpretation

Since the methodology employed participatory action research as a methodology, the fieldwork was not restricted to one interaction with the participants / sample. Instead, an on-going interaction carried on for a whole month both in formal and informal settings. To be able to answer the research question, I will use two approaches in analysing the outcomes of the participatory media development workshop. The first approach will be Group work where horizontal one-on-one communication existed both amongst the participants as well as the facilitator and interpreter. The second approach is semi-ethnographic observations in the form of informal diary and field notes.

By looking at these two approaches, the aim is to give an all round interpretation and analysis of the available data. The risk of overlooking potentially useful and crucial information would creep in if just one of the approaches were used. Moreover, the study could thus exploit the potential of all the rich data available to make more concise and well-informed conclusions.

Given below are a number of quotes and observations that the researcher considers most relevant from the various activities that were focussed towards finding answers towards this particular research question. Due to the enormity of the available data, I audiotaped all the sessions and used the tapes and diary-notes as points of reference rather than transcribing 30 days worth of workshop activity. Only the most interesting activities were transcribed. Appendix 1 is one of these activities. Using the discussions and personal observations as the base, certain recurrent strong themes emerged. A 'theme' was concluded only when a number of children expressed same thoughts either in formal or informal settings. The reasoning behind these conclusions, therefore, is, the frequency and firmness with which these ideas were put forth.

Having spent 30 full days with the children, the researcher was in a position to understand some of the perspectives that the participants spoke from. The methodological accuracy of such an approach could be disputed. Would it be possible to generalise these findings to all the children in Afghanistan? That is something that would require further research. Since it was the policy of the organisation to not question the social background of the children, it was impossible to understand where they came from. However, this research gives a fantastic insight into the world of the Afghan children.

Emergent Themes

Reviewed below are some of the themes that emerged out of the interaction with the children. The interpretations are supplemented with scenarios, quotes that substantiate the drawn conclusions.

a) Popular Culture:

As detailed above in the tabular column, the group work consisted of everyday workshops where the children thought about different aspects of community media creation and were involved in a pedagogic process to develop skills required to achieve the same.

The first week consisted of activities in which ice-breaking activities were conducted. Games such as 20 questions were conducted as a way to get to know each other. One group member was chosen to think of a famous personality and the rest of the group were to guess the personality with 20 questions that could only be answered with a 'Yes' or 'No'. There was only time for two rounds of the game before switching to other games. The two personalities that the participants thought of were Rafi Naabzada and Hamid Karzai. It took less than 10 questions for the other participants to guess both these personalities. It wasn't very difficult for the children to guess – as if they knew.

Rafi Naabzada is the winner of the first season of 'Afghan Star' – a reality show based on American Idol, where singers from across the country contest for the top title. Hamid Karzai, the President of the country was the choice in the second round.

Later, I learnt that Rafi Naabzada was immensely popular and most children watched the program on Tolo TV. Even the children who didn't have TV sets at home went to their friends' or relatives' houses to make sure they didn't miss the program.

The observations in the 20 songs activity imply that the participants adore the emergent music scene in Afghanistan. In a country where music was banned for almost eight years during the Taliban regime, the new influx of Afghan singers help foster a national identity. The reference to the 'Afghan Star' program is another glaring example of how important these children consider music to be in their lives.

While Bollywood music is still popular and many children can sing songs from Urdu movies, they displayed a very close affection to Afghan songs in their own languages. Songs, both in Dari and Pashto are hugely popular amongst the young and the old alike.

Diary Entry – Aug 3, 2010

"Today Fazila sang me a song. She has an amazing voice. She says when she was a baby no music was allowed in the country. The Taliban didn't like music, she reasoned. She didn't remember anything unusual. "I never knew about singing. But now I hear songs from India all the time. I love Bollywood songs. Amitabh Bachchan, oh my favourite! He is so good and handsome. It is so nice this Indian music. I want to go see India once. It seems so nice and has all the beautiful people," she said. She sang me a song about love and loneliness. She didn't know what it meant, but she knew all the words and sang it with the precision of a professional."

While Bollywood music is perceived as a 'far-off dream', Afghan music is considered something they can relate and something they can be proud of. Also, the winner of the reality show is considered an idol by the children of Afghanistan. Many of them expressed a wish to be part of the program so they could be 'famous' and 'inspirational' to other people across Afghanistan.

Shafeeq Mureed, one of the most popular singers who shot to national fame after his song on Afghan nationalism is a clear evidence to prove this.

They were all very proud to have shown me, a foreigner, that their own culture wasn't any behind and that they had their own stars and didn't have to depend on 'foreign stars' anymore.

Diary Entry – Aug 14, 2010

"Today the children went to attend a video shoot. They were all super-excited. They couldn't wait to get out of our magazine sessions. They were fully distracted and kept whispering to each other. They were all very excited to go watch Shafeeq Mureed shoot. Some of the children are starring in his next music video. One of them made me listen to one of his songs on their mobile phone. I didn't think it was very good, but they all love him. When I asked them why they all liked him so much, they said that his music was amazing and they particularly liked one of his other songs invoked nationalistic feelings. They were in awe of the music video which showed different landscapes of Afghanistan and also feature children in it."

Shafeeq Mureed, one of the leading pop stars in Afghanistan, shot to national fame after his song on Afghan nationalism was released. The children listened to Shafeeq Mureed songs a lot and treated him as their idol. While Indian and Iranian media is still the most popular, the local Afghan music scene is playing a crucial role in shaping the national identities of the children. It wouldn't be wrong to say, at the time of this study, popular youth media in Afghanistan is synonymous to the local Afghan pop culture. This trend will probably continue in the coming years and spill over to the film industry and other mainstream media. Creating this magazine gave the children the same pride they attached to watching Rafi Naabzada sing on 'Afghan Star'. A sense of belonging and togetherness is what these children seem to be searching for. And in current-day Afghanistan media seems to be carrying out this role very effectively.

b) Religion:

Diary Entry, Aug 7th, 2010

"The children asked me about why I did not cover my head like the women in the Indian serials. They knew that women in Bollywood movies didn't really cover their heads, but, they were women in the cinemas. The women in the soap operas were more real, and they all covered their heads. Why then did I not cover my head in the photos I showed them on my mobile phone, they wondered. They also asked me if I was only covering my head because I was in Afghanistan. Didn't women in London cover their heads, they questioned. They then concluded that the culture was different. Yes, they had seen white women on TV and newspapers who didn't really cover their head. "In Afghanistan, a girl who didn't cover her head is just bad. Islam won't allow it," said Shamila.

Most of the children's perception about morality can be traced back to their religion. They constantly judge all foreign content they are exposed to with Islam as the basis. The women on Indian soap-operas, for instance were considered more Islamic (due to the cultural similarities), than women in English language movies. Most of the children seemed to be in a dilemma regarding the path of Islam they should follow.

"The most important thing about any kind of children's media is that it should help us know more about our religion. It should teach us Islamic religious way of life and what is correct and not correct. Sometimes there are so many people saying bad things about Islam. Like Taliban. They are saying, 'In the name of Allah', but they are killing and doing harm and that is not Islam. So we want to know what is the correct way of life."

Nabi Amin (m), 12 – Good Media / Bad Media Activity

Afghanistan is a society in transition from a totalitarian regime to a current-day moderate government. While most children acknowledged that extremism and violence was wrong, they were not sure how to deal with softer issues such as gender equality, pluralism and questioning adults. While they knew that Islam's ideas on these issues was slightly contradictory to what they were being exposed to via western NGOs and all the rights education work that is being carried on in Afghanistan, many of them sought the magazine and the media as a means to clarify and renegotiate what they were being taught at home as the right way of thinking. The children were never exposed to free-thinking and were always used to having someone tell them what to think. This was where the request for 'advice' columns in the magazine came from. With most of the Afghan media addressing religious issues in some, if not all programming, and almost always with varying intensities, the children seem to be at a crossroads in deciding their religious beliefs.

c) Conflict and Politics:

The representation activity was one in which the children were made to think about how the international media portrayed them, what was right or wrong about it, how they would change it and why. They were further asked to reflect about how they would want the represent themselves in the magazine. A set of nine photos were selected by the children themselves using the internet. They were divided into two groups.

"The photos show that the children are in a bad situation, affected by war. It is not good. It is very bad and it is a sad situation. Some of the photos show that the children could not go to school, they are working on the streets, disabled. These types of photos are very boring for us. We don't like looking at them. The infrastructure is destroyed and children are orphaned. It was not a good way to show Afghan children. We hate war and we don't want it again. It is very boring to see images of war. Afghanistan has a good future and I don't think the foreigners know about this. How can they know? If this is what they see, then they will think all children in Afghanistan are like this, they are weak and helpless. But look at us, you should go and tell your friends in London. We are not weak or helpless. They are just unaware."

Manija (f), 12, Representation Activity

"They are showing children like this. But they don't know many things about Afghan children. In Iran, they are giving narcotics to the children. I don't know why. But when we were in Iran, my mother always used to tell me not to talk to strangers. They make them work after giving them narcotics. Even here, they give it to babies, in the villages and make them sleep. They don't cry if they are given narcotics, so the parents don't have to feed them. The

foreigners don't know about this and the media is not telling them. I think the media for foreigners should have this and they should help Afghan children. But not in our magazine. Because we don't want to know about these things. It is making us sad."

Sahar (f), 12, Representation Activity

"I think the foreigners should not look at these photos and think negative about us. There are lot of talented Afghan children and the media should show about some of the talented children and not show these sad and boring images. I feel like crying when I see it. I don't want to. Maybe we can send our magazine to other children in other countries and show them that we are not like this, always fighting."

Rumal (m), 15, Representation Activity

"It should be something that should not talk about war and politics. Children hate talking about war or politics. This war story makes us very sad. And sometimes I cry when I see the dead people's news on TV. We all want happy stories in the magazine. War and Politics is for the older people. Not for us children. It is not good and we should not think about it."

Fazila (f), 15, Good media / Bad Media Activity

As noted in the quotes, all the children in the workshop categorically rejected wanting to speak about conflict or politics. They called it boring and topics that only adults deserved to discuss. While doing the representation activity, where the children were shown photos of other children from conflict zones, almost all of them had tears in their eyes. They all said that they didn't want to discuss anything about their lives from the past because it made them feel distressed. Anything that discussed conflict in the media, according to them, wasn't developed for children. Many of them questioned why it was necessary to talk about war when it was over and there was peace again. However, they also did acknowledge there was still fighting going on in many parts of the country. But they all thought that even the children in conflict zones would like to read a magazine that focussed more on other issues than war or politics. While politics and conflict seem to be popular topics that they encounter in their everyday life, they seem to want to distance themselves as far as possible from these issues. However, this did not mean that they weren't interested in child rights issues. They were well aware that the war brought in all kinds of problems for children. One of the activities involved asking the children draw about the problems children faced in Afghanistan and many drew pictures with recurring themes of poverty, child labour and landmine related accidents. When questioned how this could be solved, they all said it had to change from the government.

However, over the course of the workshop, the content that the children developed suggested that they didn't expect the government to come up with any kind of drastic development initiatives. Instead, they suggested ways to use peer power to improve their lives. For instance, in the drama workshop, the core theme that the children wanted to address was the lack of teachers in schools. The conclusion for the story they came up with suggests that the protagonists and the antagonists, instead of fighting with each other should help each other in their academic work to be able to tackle the problem of teacher incompetency. This essentially also means that the children didn't really think that it was possible for the government to take initiatives to address the problem. Similarly, in the agony aunt column, one of the questions post by a child was how her neighbour could learn to read and write, since her parents wouldn't allow her to go to school. Similar responses were given by the rest of the participants, where she was expected to seek the help of friends and family to learn to read and write. They didn't think that the political system of capable of intervening and helping her at all.

In essence, the children perceive politics and conflict to be something that doesn't necessarily inhabit their world. They see it as something that they have little control over and something that has little control over how they live their lives. By ignoring it, they assume that it doesn't exist and hence that it doesn't affect their lives.

d) Framing Gender:

"Girls don't get break time in school. Some girls' schools have break-time but many don't. Even in break-time, my teacher doesn't allow me to play. They only ask us to sit and do needle-work because she says it will be useful when I grow up. (Needle-work is considered an essential skill, just like cooking and cleaning for to-be brides). If there are some games in the magazine, then I can just sit quietly and play in the magazine and the teacher or parents won't be angry. Running and playing is what boys do.

Zahraw (f), 11, Drama Workshop

A brief flip through the magazine will immediately suggest the dominance of the female form. While there were equal number of male and female participants in the workshop, all the male participants acknowledged that the girls in the group were less privileged than the boys in terms of opportunities in general. However, the boys in the group always considered themselves superior to the girls. Though they were very wary of displaying this behaviour in front of me, it was quite evident in the classroom activities. The girls were the ones who always cleaned the hall after the sessions. The girls fetched water, while the boys carried the stationary tubs. However, this behaviour changed after the first few days when I encouraged both sexes to involve in the chores.

One of the activities involved reading a passage in English (all students studied English as a second language in school. However their level of competency remained very low), understanding and explaining it to the rest of the class. They all read passages from their English text books. One of the passages spoke about children and their families. The passage described about how men in the family 'drank tea and talked to each other' and women 'knitted and did domestic chores'. These kind of gendered frameworks are commonplace and there is little or no debate on the authenticity of the same. Young boys are taught that their role would be that of a bread-winner and young girls, that of a home-maker. It is difficult for them to think of it any other way. In the last week, three girls came up to me and said that they wanted to be journalists when they grew up. They said that they wanted to be like me, 'brave' and 'independent'. However, they also said that their communities were very orthodox and would never allow it. The same girls, during the ice-breaker activities all said that they wanted to be housewives. My role as a facilitator can be relative to what we term 'communicative media'. My role as a facilitator, was used as a medium to communicate identities of gender that they had never experienced first-hand before. As one of the children referred (as quoted above), the women in Bollywood didn't cover their heads and hence they weren't moral. However, in my contact with them, they came to understand that I didn't cover my head either. However, having known me personally, they realised that I wasn't really an immoral person. This along many other notions of femininity I communicated through my role as a facilitator were very different from what they were used to. Their only reasoning was that the culture was different. However, they still weren't ready to challenge the established norms of gender amongst themselves.

"Kyunki Saas Bhi Kabhi Bahi Thi (Because even the mother-in-law was a daughter-in-law once), which is a very popular serial in India is being broadcast here in Afghanistan. What the former UN under Seceretary-General, Sashi Tharoor referred to as 'soft power' from Bollywood, is being felt in this country. Rumal today told me that the broadcast timings had to be changed for the serial, because the Mullahs got really angry that people didn't turn up to the mosques for prayers. They all chose to watch the soap instead. One of the children today told me that women in Indian serials served their men and were generally demure, just like a good Afghan woman would be. This is why they liked Indian women, he said. He went on to wonder why I was not married and how it was possible for me to travel to a different country all by myself. Why was I not like one of the women in the serial? He wondered. How had my parents allowed me to come?"

Diary Entry, July 27, 2010

The children of Afghanistan are exposed to multiple forms of gender construction through the media with the influx of Pakistani, Indian, American, Iranian and Turkish content filtering into the country. This brings us back to the debate on the public sphere and how the children have been denied their space in it. It appears that they would want to use the magazine, their alternative media space to negotiate these multiple notions of gender and identity from their own point of view, and not necessarily from that of an adult. The story that the children came up with during the drama workshop perpetuates feminine stereotypes where the girls are kind and caring towards the erring male antagonist. However, the interview with Palwasha, a 12 year old girl and the winner of a national juggling contest, pushes these limits and experiments with redefining traditionally gendered functions.

Even though there was a male winner and a female winner for the juggling contest, the children insisted that the female be chosen for the interview, because they believed that there were very few opportunities for girls and that she could prove an inspiration to a number of other children. Allowing this sort of enquiry, would be the first step towards bringing about any kind of gender equality in Afghanistan.

e) Edutainment. Colour. Fun:

One of the other activities that we did during the workshop was to think about what made good children's media. We did this activity with the aid of 'Parwaz' – a children's magazine that was published back in 2002 by AINA, an organization that works for education of children and women. However, they stopped publishing after a couple of issues.

Parwaz, which means to fly, was the first and only children's magazine in Afghansitan. The participants were asked to look at the magazine and asked come up with a list of what they liked about the magazine. Once they did this, the workshop progressed to the next level, where they were asked to think about what would make good children's media and what would make bad children's media. The participants worked in 4 groups here are some excerpts from what they came up with.

"What I like about Parwaz is that they have something about every subject from school. I wish they still printed it. But now we have our magazine and I think we are going to be better than them. I really like the jokes and funny pictures they have in the book (referring to a translated TinTin comic-strip) I just want something that I can see and laugh and laugh so I am happy. In school the teachers are always scolding and beating us. If I can see the magazine and smile for sometime, then I can forget about my problems for a while."

Samiullah (m), 12

"It should have lot of advice from the elders and it should teach us how to improve ourselves. We can be good children by knowing these things. I also want to learn about how the famous people become famous. How can one be successful?"

Firomarz (m), 16, Kabul

"The media that is good is not available on TV or newspapers. There is nothing for children in Afghanistan. Even in TV or radio, only some time is given for children and that is also not nice. They show cartoons sometimes dubbed in Dari and we like it. If it is colorful, and funny and has lot of cartoons, then I will love it so much."

Sahar (f), 12, Favourite TV Program Activity

"This afternoon we went to visit the girls' school. Rukshana High School in Kabul is one of the many funded by UNICEF. The children showed me how they had earlier decided that they wanted more friendly and colourful school spaces in one of the children's parliament session. Consequently, they spent time painting and decorating the school. Most of the paintings involved birds, children and Islamic symbols. When asked, they said that they wanted their paintings to represent peace and joy in their learning environment. They said they loved colours. Manija said that her neighbour was very jealous of her because she went to a school that had so many paintings and colours. They all love school."

Diary Entry, 20 Aug, 2010

"Today the children spoke about how important was for them in the national Shura-e-Atfal. It was amazing how all the kids unanimously considered education the most important parts of their lives. Many children even opined that having breaks in school would mean lack of precious study time!"

Diary Entry, 7 Aug, 2010

Most children expressed the need to feel to see content that wasn't dull and boring. They wanted colour and lots of it. This also reflected in the school re-decoration project that they did. They loved everything that was bright. Like children around the world, Afghan children enjoy colour too. In the workshops, they said they like looking at colourful pictures and that it made them laugh.

All of their text books. the only kind of reading material, many of them were exposed to, were black and white and hardly had any pictures. The pictures they saw were all from adult magazines / foreign language publications. Many NGOs use pictorial representations to increase awareness on various issues. Since the children in Afghanistan don't start school until they are seven, and even when they do, have very bad teachers, they tend to be weak in reading comprehension.

This can be argued as one of the reasons for their liking to pictures and colour. What the children meant by pictures and colour can be given a deeper reading to interpret 'joy' and 'happiness'. They associated colour with happiness and wanted their magazine to be a happy place. Most children seemed to associate good behaviour with good academics. Many of them even said that break-time in school should not be given because it would encroach upon their study time. Education is highly regarded amongst all the children. They know that it is attributed to good conduct and sincerity. It was a righteous way of life. The display of dichotomy was particularly interesting to observe. The good child studied, behaved well and was religious, while the bad child was irreligious, careless and badly behaved. There hardly existed a middle ground in their interpretations.

This notion spilled on to the content of the book which includes several pieces of Islamic content. There is an Islamic story, a scanned calligraphy of a koranic phrase, a colouring corner that shows the image of a Muslim woman praying with her son, an article about Haj and an amazing fact about the largest clock in the world, situated in Mecca.

Similarly, the amazing facts page spoke about facts from science. There was also a separate section on butterflies (again science). The children place a lot of emphasis on learning and expect the magazine to be a portal to enrich their knowledge.

But they also want to balance work with play. But however, playing is seen as something that is unnecessary and only one that is done by children who are not 'good'. To solve this problem, they suggested including games that required thinking. Some riddles and a game of Sudoku was included for this. However, they did go on and contradict themselves by including a board game of snakes and ladders, a game that is played purely by chance.

Like we'll discuss below, the children were constantly restructuring their identities to suit their likes. Many of them were torn apart between choosing to be what the social norms expected them to be and what they felt happy doing. The media space is just another tool to allow them to continue this deliberative process.

f) Identity:

Most of the children hated the photos from the representation activity. They said that the outside world had a very wrong notion of what Afghan children were like. However, like Gender, the question of identity for the Afghan children is also on the crossroads. A few of the children in the workshop returned either from Iran or Pakistan as repatriated refugees. They spoke Farsi and Urdu, respectively. One child said that he didn't really like it here and missed his friends in Pakistan. However, another participant was quick to admonish him and tell him that he ought to be proud of his nation. While all the children said they loved Afghanistan, it also appeared as something that they said only because it was expected of them. A sense of quasi-nationalism is being built in the nation's post-conflict peace-building agenda. And the media has a major role to play in it.

The protagonist in the story from the drama workshop is a girl who returns from Iran. She complains to her friend about how the schooling system back home was much better and she found it very difficult to cope because Afghanistan didn't have good teachers. It is very interesting how the children played with this character sketch. The protagonist can be viewed as one who is facing the exact same dilemmas that the children of Afghanistan are currently going through. There were two other sections in the magazine that probe into the lives of children in other parts of the world. One is a feature about children from four different countries in the world, their photographs, their currency, capital city and language. The content instructed how to say Hello in each of the four languages. The second one was a feature on how a character named Samira, taught the children how to say their names in five different languages.

"In our schools and all the NGOs in our country talk about children's rights. We know we have our rights just like adults. If we have a children's magazine, it has to have children's issues. Just like adult magazine has adult issues. I think it will be a good idea to reach some children in rural areas by magazine. Because not all children can participate in the Shura. By writing letters to the magazine, they can tell their opinion."

Rumal (m), 16, Kabul

There is a lot of curiosity on how children in other parts of the world lived their lives. However, there is a visible uncertainty in whether or not they should apply those ways to their own lives. Again, the question of religion creeps in and a large reason for this debate would remain ethical and moral implications that they might have to face from the community.

From the definitions they came up with from the representation activity, it can be inferred that all the children knew how the world and Afghans themselves perceived the them, the children. However, they hate to be associated with it and do not want to be slotted into that stereotype.

Their approach to media signifies that they are trying to break out of the mould that the international and local media had set for them and are attempting to find new definitions to their brand new lives as post-conflict Afghan children. While this deliberative process is a continuous one, they seem to be using the alternative media space to explore some of these paradigms.

While the project began with the notion of creating an alternative media space for the children to express and represent themselves.

Chapter v

Conclusion

In essence, to trace back the research question the methodology employed in the research gave sufficient space to engage with the children of Afghanistan and understand how they look at and define children's media. The literature reviewed for this thesis suggested that children, especially in conflict and post-conflict zones have very little space in the public sphere. This leads to marginalisation of their voices hence a roadblock in the peace-building process. To make way for the voices of children to be heard, community and alternative media with a participatory communication approach is suggested as a means to allow them create their own narratives about life and society.

From the research carried out, the dominant themes that emerged regarding how the participants defined children's media and saw its their role in their lives are listed below

The children of Afghanistan consider good children's media to:

Be Islamic: To be able to help them negotiate with dilemmas surrounding personal positioning of their idea of Islam. Between the plentiful discourses of radical and moderate Islam, they expect good children's media to be able to help them decide what the right way to think would be.

Help them reframe traditionally gendered identities: As with Islam, the post-Taliban state is going through a massive surge in political rights. As it is evident from the content created by the children, they are pushing the accepted roles attributed to the sexes and exploring newer (and sometimes, more western) concepts of gender equality. They except the media to aid them explore these newly rising paradigms.

Help develop nationalistic pride: This is a very interesting phenomenon, but one that requires deeper enquiry and more research. But pop-culture and emerging media (both mainstream and alternative) seems to be taking on the role in Afghanistan. The local Afghan music scene is proving to be a tool to unite children from all over the country. The magazine itself had sections that spoke about children from parts of the country. This kind of exploration is one that is nascent and will see a lot of growth in the years to come.

Move forward from the conflict-ridden past: All the children unanimously hated images of conflict and war. They considered it to be a thing of the past and wanted to start afresh. Besides, they all expressed sadness and distress when speaking about conflict related issues. The children considered children's media as one that did not talk about anything negative but one that gave out a lot of optimistic messages. They said that they didn't identify conflict and politics as children's issues. However, they all expressed keen interest in child rights and developing knowledge on the role of children in democracy. They expected children's media to give them an outlet to express their voices and assert their rapidly evolving identities.

Reconstructing identities: The children of Afghanistan are not comfortable associating themselves with the their conflict-ridden past. While many children (especially repatriated refugees) displayed ambiguity in their liking towards the country, all of them were proud to be Afghan. However, they want to reconstruct new identities that removed them from the light of a 'conflict-affected child' to that of a 'normal child'. In some instances, they even seemed ashamed to be associated with their past and associated it with words such as 'dirty', 'lazy' and 'poor'. The alternative media space will prove to be a space where they can explore these newly emerging identities.

Fun and colour: All the children showed a keen love for colour, games and fun. But a deeper reading would mean that they all were interested in seeing more positive and happy content. Cartoons and photos were well-loved. Many mentioned that they would just look at the pictures even if they didn't understand the text. Looking at colourful designs made them happy, they said. The children expected children's media to be something that was full of this.

In essence, the children of Afghanistan defined children's media as one that was fun, entertaining and educative. They see it's role in their lives as one that will help them reconstruct the many the evolving social constructs surrounding social life.

Bibliography

Anyaegbunam, C. (1998). Participatory Rural Communication Appraisal: Starting with teh people. . Harare, Zimbabwe

Baitenmann, H. (1990). "NGOs and the Afghan War: The Politicisation of Humanitarian Aid." Third World Quarterly 12(1): 62-85.

BBCNews (2010). Afghanistan Timeline: A Chronology of Key Events. London, BBC Monitoring: BBC South Asia country profiles.

Bessette, G. (2004). Involving the Community: A guide to Participatory Development Communication. Penang, Malaysia, International Development Research Centre.

Carlsson, U. (2005). From NWICO to Global Governance of the information society. Media and Glocal Change: Rethinking Communication for Development
O. Hemer... Buenos Aires, Argentina, CLASCO: 193-214.

Darvin, J. (2009). "Make books, not war: workshops at a summer camp in Bosnia." Literacy 43(1): 50-59.

Dueze, M. (2006). "Ethnic Media, Community Media and Participatory Culture." Journalism 7(3): 262-280.

Freire, P. (1973 / 2003). Extension or Communication? Santiago / Seabury, Institute for Agricultural Reform (Spanish) / Education for Critical Consciousness (English).

Friere, P. (1997). Pedagogy of the Oppressed. New York, NY, Continuum.

Goodson, L. P. (2001). Afghanistan's endless war: state failure, regional politics, and the rise of the Talibam, University of Washington Press.

Habermas, J. (1974). "The Public Sphere: An Encyclopedia Article." New German Critique 3: 49-55.

Hamelink, C. J. (1994). Communication and Human Values. The Politics of World Communication: A human rights perspective Sage. 20: 132-149.

Hornik, R. C. (1998). Development Communication: Information, Agriculture and Nutrition in teh Third World. Lanham, MD, University Press of America.

Howley, K. (2005). Community Media: People, Places and Communication Technologies, Cambridge University Press: 1-13.

Jaffe, D. (1998). Levels of Socio-Economic Development Theory. Connecticut Praeger.

Lasweel, H. (1948). The Communication of Ideas. A series of Adresses. L. Bryson. New York, NY, Institute for Religious and Social Studies (Harper): 37-51.

Lemish, D. (2007). Why study children and media at times of conflict and war? Children and Media in Times of War and Conflict, Hampton Press: 1-12.

Lerner, D. (1958). The passing of Traditional Society. New York, NY, Free Press.

Macbride, S. (1980). Many Voices, One World: Communication and Society Today and Tomorrow - Towards a new more just and more efficient world information and communication order, International Commission for the Study of Communication Problems.

Machel, G. (1996). Promotion and Protection of the Rights of Children: Impact of armed conclict on children, United Nations.

Manyozo, L. (2006). "Manifesto for Development Communication: Nora Quebral and the Los Banos School of Development Communication." Asian Journal of Communication 16(1): 79-99.

Mckee, N. (1994). A Community-Based Learning Approach: Beyond Social Marketing:. Participatory Communication: Working for Change and Development. S. White: 194-228.

Mefalopulos, P. (2003). Theory and Practice of Participatory Communication: The case of the FAO Project "Communication for Development in Southern Africa", The University of Texas, Austin.

Melkote, S. (1991). Communication for Development in the Third World: Theory and Practice. New Delhi, India, Sage

Mouffe, C. (1998). "Deliberative Democracy or Agonistic Plurarlism " Dialogue International Edition(07-08): 9-12.

Rodriguez, C. (2001). From Alternative Media to Citizen's Media. In the Mediascape: An International Study of Citizen's Media. NJ: Hampton, Creskill: 1-24.

Rogers, E. (1960). Diffusion of Innovations. New York, Free Press.

Roozemond, N. (2002). "We Like Good Disco: The Public Sphere of Children and Its Implications for Practice " Applied Theatre Researcher 3: 1-8.

Ross, H. (2002). An operational framework for media and peacebuilding. Vancouver, B.C., IMPACS - Institute for Media, Policy and Civil Society.

Sawhney, N. (2010). "Voices Beyond Walls." 2010, from http://voicesbeyondwalls.blogspot.com

Schramm, W. (1964). Mass Media and National Development. Stanford, CA, Stanford University Press.

Skaine, R. (2002). The women of Afghanistan under the Taliban, McFarland: 61-66

Tufte..., T. (2009). Participatory Communication: A practical guide. Washington, D.C., The World Bank.

Wardell, S. B. G. (2002`). "Exploited by Who? An alternative perspective on humanitarian assistance to Afghan women." Third World Quarterly 23(No.5): 909-930.

Appendix 1 - List of Participants

1. Rumal Nabizayed, Age 16, Kabul Province (Interpreter)
2. Manija Naiemi, Age 12, Kabul Province
3. Shamila Khalagiar, Age 16, Kabul Province

4. Fazila Amarkhail, Age 15, Kabul Province
5. Samiullah Rasuli, Age 12, Bamyan Province
6. Brushna Amarkhail, Age 13, Kabul Province
7. Sahar Mohammadi, Age 12, Herat Province
8. Akhter Ansari, Age 15, Bamyan Province
9. Firomarz, Age 16, Ghor Province
10. Nabi Amin, Age 12, Nangahar Province
11. Hanon Ansari, Age 16, Bamyan Province
12. Tahira, Age 16, Kabul province
13. Khushbhu, Age 14, Herat province
14. Zahraw Kozimi, Age 11, Herat province

Appendix 2 – Workshop Schedule

Day 1 – Friday	Holiday
Day 2 – Saturday	Tour around the campus and tea meeting
Day 3 - Sunday	Writing on the wall – Art about anything
Day 4 – Monday	Ice breaker – Games and snacks
Day 6 – Tuesday	Craft shop – from carbon to golden
Day 7 – Wednesday	Theatre workshop
Day 8 – Thursday	What's your favourite media? Discussing favourite media and why
Day 9 – Friday	Holiday

Day 10 – Saturday	Representation activity – How does the international media view Afghan children?
Day 11 – Sunday	Good media / Bad Media – What in your opinion are characteristics of good and bad media? Discuss
Day 12 - Monday	Name game and Logo design workshop – Keeping in mind with the previous week's activities, come up with a name for magazine
Day 13 - Tuesday	Logo making – Hands on – Drawing, Scanning, Digitizing
Day 14 – Wednesday	Content plan – Coming up with content ideas
Day 15 – Thursday	Finalizing the content plan and assigning roles and responsibilities
Day 16 – Friday	Holiday
Day 17 – Saturday	National Theatre Festival – child reporters cover the event
Day 18 – Sunday	National Theatre Festival – child reporters cover the event
Day 19 - Monday	National Juggling Championship – child reporters cover the event
Day 20 – Tuesday	National Shura-e-Atfal
Day 21 – Wednesday	Drama workshop – Creating a story
Day 22 – Thursday	Drama workshop – Creating a story / Interview with winner of juggling championship
Day 23 – Friday	Holiday
Day 24 – Saturday	Journalism workshop – 1 – Writing and Editing
Day 25 – Sunday	Journalism workshop -2 – Writing and Editing

Day 26 – Monday	Design process begins
Day 27 – Tuesday	Full day design workshop
Day 28 – Wednesday	Full day design workshop – Dummy magazine ready

1

1

Appendix 3 - Workshop on representation

NOTE: The permission of all the children was sought before using their names.

Abbreviations:

F: Facilitator
I: Interpreter

F: Hello! Good morning!
I: (Dari)
Participants (Group): Subha Khayir (Good morning)
F: Good morning! How are you today
Knock on the door
Another participant arrives late
Children: (Dari)
I: They are saying B came late and so they want her to sing song
F: B you are late, please come in
I: (Dari)
Brushna: (Dari)
I: She is saying she has school
F: Oh... did you start school already? What about the others? Don't they also have school?
I: (Dari)
Manija: (Dari)
I: She is saying their school some other time
F: Ok, how many more of you have school and what are your timings?
I: Fa and S have school in morning till 12, so they can't come in morning. B have school in afternoon so she come at 3 o clock.
F: Ok that's no problem. School is very important. But we have the entire group here today.
I: (Dari)
F: So shall we start for today?
I: (Dari)
Group: Nodding and chorussing 'yes'
F: Ok! Great! Now that we know each other quite well and we also have a

plan on how we are going to make the magazine, let's try and think about what is already out there.

I: (Dari)

F: So, we spoke about a bit about media and how it is helping people who are in some other place, form ideas and opinions about people in other parts of the world. You guys spoke about what you thought of American kids and their lives. I think you were all wonderful

I: (Dari)

F: Awesome! So today, let us continue this and think some more, a little bit more, about maybe how...

(Zahraw lifts her hand)

F: Hang on Zw, let me finish first and then you can tell us what you think. Yeah, so I was saying... today we are going to try and think about how foreigners, foreigners like me, people in America, people in London and Pakistan and Iran and so many other parts of the world, think about the children in Afghanistan

I: (Dari)

F: Yes, Zw, you wanted to say something...

Zahraw(f): (Dari)

I: Zw is saying what is the... umm... connect – what connect this make with mujala (magazine).

F: Ah! Yes! Ok, so that's an excellent question. Umm... can any one in this group answer this question for Zw? We did talk a little about it earlier if you remember... Anyone?

I: (Dari)

F: Yes, Ak? Did I see you rasie your hand?

I: (Dari)

F: What is it?

I: No he was not raising hand.

F: I am quite sure I saw him raising his hand! Anyway... anyone else?

I: (Dari)

F: No one?

F: Ok, let me try explaining why we should do this activity... Umm... ok, so yesterday, in yesterday's activity, we looked at what you thought of children in some other countries. And most of you spoke about the American children. So can someone tell me where you learnt about these American children? Where did you see them? How do you know about them and what is

influencing the way you think about them? We did speak about this
yesterday… just try and recall…
I: (Dari)
F: Yeah? Anyone? Yes, Fz
Fazila: (Dari)
F: Louder, make sure that everyone in the group is able to hear you…
I: (Dari)
Fazila: (Dari)
I: Fazilaz say, she seeing the stories about American child in TV and
museum.
F: Yes! Exactly! So, many of you who have access to TV have seen what
children in foreign countries look like through the media. So maybe it is
correct to say that the media is the eye to the rest of the world? Yeah? It is
possible to see what is happening somewhere else without actually being
there. Also, most of you have had a chance to go visit the Kabul Museum and
have seen the photos clicked by children from the American exchange
program. So photos are also a form of media. Visual media, meaning
something that it speaks and gives information and understanding to our
eyes…
I: (Dari)
F: So Zw, do you now have a little idea why we are doing this exercise?
I: (Dari)
F: We are trying to think about how the rest of the world understands Afghan
children and then we are going to try and see if this matches your ideas of
what Afghan children are. Then maybe, we will see how we can implement
your ideas of what Afghan children stand for into our magazine, like we
discussed earlier. Does this sound like a good idea?
I: (Dari)

Firomarz (m): Yes, that is good idea.
F: So, how can we find out about what other people not in Afghanistan think
about us?
I: (Dari)
F: Yes, Brushna
Brushna (f): (Dari)
I: (Dari)
I: Brushna say she look at picture of Afghan child in TIME magazine.

F: Very good! That is a good way to understand how they think about us.
That is the media of the western world.
I: (Dari)
F: Ok, so let us look at some more pictures and try to analyse it.
I: (Dari)
F: Why don't you all go to the computer room, find some pictures of Afghan
children on google and bring it back? So if someone in some other country
searches for Afghan children these are the first pictures that come. So I think
it is a good way to find out what the first impressions are. What do you think?
Is that a good idea? If anyone has any other ideas of how we can do this
activity, tell us…
I: (Dari)
All the children nod.
F: Rumal will help you search on the internet. So can we say 30 mins to bring
back some pictures on the laptop?
I: (Dari)
F: Ok great!
Group breaks
Group reconvenes
F: So! Great to see you all back!
I: (Dari)
F: So do we have the pictures now?
I: (Dari)
F: Awesome, can I have a look at it?
F: that's impressive. So we have 9 photos now and they all seem to be very
interesting pictures. Now let us split into two groups and try to think about
what each photo says about Afghan children. Imagine that you are someone
who does not know what Afghanistan is like and they just see these photos
for the first time... If it were you, what would you think?
I: (Dari)
F: If you try to rub out everything that you know of Afghanistan, and try and
look at the photos with a new eye, how would you think of Afghan children.
Let us think about this now…
I: (Dari)
F: Shall we say fifteen mins for this nine pictures? Ideally, each of the groups
would want to think about what the picture describes, what your instant
emotions to it are, how you think someone else will think of this picture and

what it says about the conditions of Afghan children. Let us split into two groups now…
F: After you discuss, one of you from each group come and present to the group on your team's opinions…
I: (Dari)

Groups split and indulge in horizontal discussions

F: So who'd like to come and present from this group?
I: (Dari)
F: Come on Fazila…
Fazila: (Dari)
I: Fazila saying the photo with the child no legs making everyone feel so sad. It is landmine photo. Lot of baby. So many small kids in Afghanistan affect by landmine and it is making very sad.
F: Yeah, go on…
Fz: (Dari)
I: All picture showing that Afghan children badly affect by war. It is showing many children are orphan or alone… not having house and they facing bomb blast and they not having money and olders.
F: Yes, go on…
Fazila: (Dari)
I: The children sad and crying and American soldiers are there
F: So what do you think the American soldiers are doing in the pictures?
I: (Dari)
Fz: (Dari)
I: In one photo they are helping children and another twos they are doing scaring.
F: Yes, go on…do you have anything to say? Manija?
Manija: (Dari)
I: The photo is showing the children are in a bad situation, affect by war. It is not good. It is very bad and it is a sad situation. Some of the photos showing children not go school, they are working on streets, disabled. This type of photos are very boring for us. We don't like looking at them. The infrastructure is destroyed and children are orphan. It was not a good way to show Afghan children.
F: Yeah…
I: She saying… we hate war and we don't want again. It is very boring to see

images of war. Afghanistan has a good future and I don't think the foreigners know about this. How can they know? If they see this, then they think all children in Afghanistan are like this, they are weak and helpless. But look at us, you should go and tell your friends in London. We are not weak or helpless. They just don't know.

F: Yeah, go on…

Manija: (Dari)

I: She is saying that's all and it is finish.

F: Thank you very much Manija. Let's all clap for her

Clapping

F: So let's look at what the other group has to say…

I: (Dari)

F: Who is going to present?

I: (Dari)

F: Yes, Hanon

Hanon (m): (Dari)

I: They are giving in order of photo… first photo.. the childrens are alone after bomb. It is looking like Darul Aman palace.

F: hmm…

Hanon: (Dari)

I: Hanon is saying, second picture is small girl looking at police. He is holding gun. They are saying maybe she is scared.

F: Yea

Hanon: (Dari)

I: Then it is photo of American soldier protecting children again. He is asking them to come to him.

Interruption

Manija(f): (Dari)

I: M is saying it is not protecting. He is wanting shoot children. Or scaring the childrens.

F: So we have a dispute here… What is the soldier trying to do picture… do you think he is trying to protect the children or scare them?

Sahar(f): (Dari)

I: The American soldiers is nice. They are helping the chidlrens.

Nabi (m): (Dari)

I: Nabi is saying, they will not shoot the childrens. He is telling, in previous

pictures also the American soldier in being friendly with the childrens
F: Ok… what about you Manija? Does anyone else disagree with what Nabi and Sahar are saying?
M: (Dari)
I: No she is saying the soldier is pointing gun at children so children are scared. Why he is pointing gun if he wanting to protect children?
Samiullah (m): (Dari)
I: Samiullah saying the gunman is not putting gun down because he is having instruction from his senior. And if he put gun down then it is not rule of army…
F: Oh…
Samiullah: (Dari)
I: He saying, yes, the American army is never harming children.
F: So you are saying that the American army always helps children and doesn't
I: It one of American soldier protecting children. It is happy photo and the children are enjoying with him.
F: Go on…
I: (Dari)
F: Yes, Sahar, you have something more to say?
Sahar: (Dari)
I: She is saying you must not know that
F: What is it? It's ok, you can tell me.
Sahar: (Smiles)
F: Yes, go on…
Sahar: (Dari)
I: They are showing children like this. But they don't know many things about Afghan childrens. In Iran, they are giving narcotics to the children.
F: Why?
I: She say she don't know why. But when she living in Iran, her mother always telling her not talk strangers. They make them work after giving them narcotics. Even here, they give babies, in the villages for sleeping. They don't cry if they are given narcotics, so the parents don't feed them. The foreigners don't know about this and the media is not telling them. I think the media for foreigners should have this and they should help Afghan children. But not in our magazine. Because we don't want to know about these things.
Sahar: (Dari) It is making us sad.

F: So let us continue with our activity…
I: (Dari)
Hanon: (Dari)
I: The other picture is making all very sad. We don't want to look at it. It is as though fire in eyes. It is not good for us. The baby is crying and it is having no leg because of landmine.
F: How do you feel about this? Do you think it is happening a lot in Afghanistan?
Akhter (m): Yes, it is happening lot. But in village places.
I: (m): We are feeling very disturb. This photo. We can't even say anything…
F: Yes it is really terrible… and it is very sad that such a small baby is affected like this…
Shamila (f): (Dari)
I: She say, Allah will help them…
F: Yes, we hope God will shower his blessings on all of us…
F: Ok… let's move on to the next picture…
Hanon: (Dari)
I: This is maybe photo of bomb blast. And children running with bed quilt. Maybe they don't have mother father. It is looking like they are orphan… he is saying…
F: What is your reaction towards this picture? Anyone? How did you feel when you saw this picture?

Brushna (f): (Dari)
I: Brushna say, they are looking ugly, lazy and dirty. They are looking like they have to work and they don't have any father-mother. And people outside who seeing this photo think we are all like that. But Afghan children not lazy. Some children have like this problem. But what to do…
F: Yeah… let's look at our next picture…
Firomarz: (Dari)
I: The next two picture. The first is girls going to school. Then the other is where small children are crying. Alone, I think. Because they are not having their parents and house broken.
F: Do you really think the girls are going to school?
I: (Dari)
Manija (f): (Dari)
I: Yes she think they are going to school.

F: What about the broken stones there… this is actually a picture from a school explosion…
Manija: (Dari)
I: She say she think it is construction work.. and there is always building work in all schools. So Manija think it is that.
F: So now we've discussed more or less what we think about these pictures… Can we get into groups gain and write down in the charts, some keywords that explain how the foreigners will think of Afghan children as… Basically, I just want a summary of points from what we have just done…

I: (Dari)
F: So in the end, each group will put up the charts in the wall, as usual…
Class splits into 2 groups
Class reconvenes
F: So that was a good start to what we are looking at today… That was very nice… Let's see what we have…
I: They both decide to make one chart together. They saying they heard and they were writing same. So they make one chart.
F: Wow! Even better!
F: Yes, Rumal, why don't you read it out…
I: "I think the foreigners should not look at these photos and think negative about us. There are lot of talented Afghan children and the media should show about some of the talented children and not show this sad and boring images. We feel like crying when we see it. I don't want to. Maybe we can send our magazine to other children in other countries and show them that we are not like this, always fighting."
F: Yes, I am sure we can do that! Is it already? Ok, I guess we should wrap up now…
See you in the next seesion… Khuda Hafiz…
I: (Dari)
1

1

www.ingramcontent.com/pod-product-compliance
Lightning Source LLC
Chambersburg PA
CBHW031809150726
47989CB00006B/2939